DEAR BLACK GIRL, LET ME HOLD YOUR PAIN

You Can't Claim Your Power if Your Hands are Full

LYRIQUE RICHARDS

Lucky Book Publishing

To request permissions, contact the publisher at hello@luckybookpublishing.com.

Paperback ISBN: 978-1-998287-62-8
Hardcover ISBN: 978-1-998287-63-5
E-book ISBN: 978-1-998287-64-2

1st edition, March 2025

This book is dedicated to

Tey

Ajah

Tiana

Marley

Karis

Nykirah

✦ **You** ✦

MY GIFT TO YOU

I am so glad you're here!

As my Gift to you, get FREE Access to the Audiobook of
Dear Black Girl, Let Me Hold Your Pain and other bonus content by
scanning the QR Code below or visiting
lyriquerichards.ca

MY DREAM

My dream for this book is a growing one. For the young Black girls around the world, for the women, mothers, grandmothers, aunties, cousins, friends, and my family, to know that their story is important. The world tells us that no one struggles more than the Black woman, but then doesn't give us the support we need. So, Black women created their own support systems, and my dream is to play my part.

My story is not uncommon, at times the pain was subtle and at times it screamed so loud I tuned it out. All of it though, made me feel things a lot of Black girls and women do - insecure, unsure, doubtful, and ashamed. This isn't about dwelling or living in the past. It's about becoming confident in who you are *because* of all the things you've felt.

No matter where or when you read this book, I hope it inspires and empowers you. Use its pages to express how you feel and tell your story. My dream is that when you close this book, you can walk away feeling your authentic self and proud of who you are. And, when you need to, return to its pages and remind yourself of where you've been and how far you've come.

My Dear Black Girl, let's do this together. Planning an event, hosting a book club, looking for a keynote speaker, or simply wanting to share this message? I'm here for you. I would be honoured to be there! Sharing my knowledge and experience is both my passion and my purpose. If my words inspire or motivate even one person, I consider it a success.

My dream is that more of our stories get told, by our hands and our voices, so that our stamp on this world is undeniable.

Claim your space, claim your power.

lyriquerichards.ca

TABLE OF CONTENTS

PREFACE

"You may not control all the events that happen to you,
but you can decide not to be reduced by them."
– Maya Angelou

Dear Black Girl,

Our parents, friends, and loved ones tell us how beautiful and strong we are – they're right, of course. Celebrities and social media influencers give us role models to look up to. We stand in front of the mirror, for what seems like hours on end, reciting the affirmations that helped others, and that we believe, and hope, will help us too. There's nothing wrong with that. There is strength in choosing to respect and honour your beauty every day and make it a habit.

But no matter how much our parents give us confidence and reassurance, no matter how many close friends we have who love us for who we are, there are some things a young Black girl will go through. Kids are curious; they don't mean harm, but sometimes, their questions can make a young Black girl question herself. I want her to know that she is not alone.

Take my hand and walk through my life. I can guarantee we have more in common than you might think. I'm not next to you as you read, but you'll find me in the pages of this book. I'm sharing my story to give you the confidence to let it out and let it go.

After each chapter, you have the space to share your reflections and your story and to journal your thoughts and feelings so that you can lighten the load you carry. Your writing on those pages will let me hold your pain so that your hands are free to claim your power.

With love,

Lyrique Richards

CHAPTER 1
EARLY CHILDHOOD LESSONS

"Your story is what you have, what you will always have.
It is something to own."
– Michelle Obama

Something you need to know about me to frame the stories I'll tell is that I grew up in a big town with a small-town feel – Ottawa. To paint an even better picture, I grew up in the east end, in Orléans, which is very well known for being mostly white people. I'll probably make several references to Orléans and how it impacted my childhood but know that many towns in many places look just like mine.

This means that from a very young age I was very aware of my Blackness. I knew that my peers likely didn't listen to the same kind of music that filled my home – calypso, soca, reggae, dancehall; wouldn't understand the Caribbean slang of my family or the "broughtupsy" my culture and heritage instilled in me. Looking back, I could have been one of the first Black kids who kids my age met. And that was in the early 2000s.

My Broughtupsy Checklist

✔ Say "good morning," "afternoon," or "good evening" when greeting others

✔ Look people in the eye when talking to them

✔ Eat with a knife, fork, and napkin

✔ No elbows on the table

✔ Wait to eat until everyone at the table has their food

✔ Don't go upstairs in someone's house unless invited

✔ Don't whistle indoors

✔ Don't wear a hat indoors

✔ And more...

I was lucky: the second born. My brother, two years older than me, went through all this first. He taught my parents how to navigate parenting a school-age Black kid at a primarily white school, and he laid a path for me to follow.

Let's rewind. My name is Lyrique Richards. My parents are immigrants from Jamaica and Antigua. They came to Canada each around the age of 12 and had hard experiences on the brink of their teenhood. They learned to cope and survive. And those are the lessons they passed to my brother and me.

Code-Switching 101

I didn't know the word for it of course, because I was so young, but whether they intended to or not, my parents taught me how to code-switch. I learned that in a group of white people, there's a certain way I should talk, walk, and look. And there are different reasons for that. Something about Caribbean people, if you don't know, is that they care deeply about image. Making sure you look proper before leaving the house, even if that's just crossing the street to get the mail. So, code-switching was a way to show the white people that we cannot be looked down on if we look and sound our best.

To "study" how to interact with my new white friends and schoolmates, I started to listen to rock, pop, and country. Not that I would make it known, but I would analyze what they wore and try to replicate it with my closet. I would style my braids to emulate their hairstyles. And I would rarely talk about my culture.

There's another level to this too. My best friend (for context, she's white) reminds me of a time when we were in third grade. I don't remember exactly what our teacher asked us, but I raised my hand in class and shared with everyone some of the things my parents told me every day before leaving the house on how to behave in public. And something I said really stood out to her: "When indoors or in a store, especially, never have your hands in your pockets, and never wear a hood." She told me this stuck with her, even to this day. She didn't realize how much I had to think about at such a young age when we'd go shopping together.

Though no one and certainly no kid should ever have to code-switch, I'm grateful for the lesson. I saw how the kids who were slightly different were treated, how the kids who didn't have the latest trends and fashions were ridiculed, and I'd be writing a very different book if that were my story. My parents taught me how to cope and survive.

My Dear Black Girl,

If you've ever had to code-switch, you know that it can get exhausting. You can lose yourself. You don't need to shed your culture to fit in because, *and I'm letting you in on a secret here*... Everyone is looking to fit in. Define what is meaningful to you, what represents you, and know how your authenticity lights up any room you enter; write a new code.

The Second-Generation Experience

I carried my culture with me every day, and still do, though the degree to which I would share outwardly with pride has evolved – being Caribbean is the essence of who I am. I know that my new code is to share the art, music, food, stories, clothes, and yes, broughtupsy with my little cousins (and trust me there's a lot of us, if you know my family) and with you, my little sister.

When I introduced myself earlier, I told you that my parents came to Canada from Jamaica and Antigua. Since my parents immigrated to Canada, it makes my brother and me second-generation Canadians. Mom and Dad learned quickly how to fit in here. Once they found each other, they moved in together, got married, had my brother, bought a house, and had me. In my earliest memory, I'm sitting in the living room of the first house I lived at, in Orléans, playing with my cat, Tiger Stripes, and watching TV; if I think harder, my dad is probably playing some reggae on his speaker system and my mom is braiding my hair. I thought nothing of it, and that's the way my parents wanted it to be.

But when I was about 10 years old, we moved to Paradise, and you'll get the irony of that real soon. Paradise ripped off my rose-coloured glasses. I learned what it meant to be an immigrant and what it meant to be a Black family in a white neighbourhood. It was my parents' third home at that point, so they weren't new to homeownership. Later in life, my dad told me how often he was asked how much his rent is, or how long he's renting the home for; no one believed he could be a homeowner. And, when we moved from Paradise and into a new home, my dad was asked by a new neighbour if he'd ever owned a home before. Because of comments like those, my brother and I were taught how to play.

Let me explain.

My parents made sure that my brother and I weren't the "rowdy" neighbourhood kids. Made sure we weren't yelling too loud, playing too close to other people's houses, playing music too loud, and also made sure our yard was always clean. I never thought they were strict – it was my normal. But sometimes my friends thought differently. I know my parents were worried about how the neighbours would see us. And they made sure no one could ever say, "Damn those loud kids," "I don't want you going to their house," or "Can you please handle your children?" Translation: "You're the crazy, loud, Black family."

At Paradise, we were still given plenty, all the latest toys. I especially loved my Skip It. We had a black boombox in the garage which my dad would use to play the local Caribbean radio station as we played. I remember the drainage on the street wasn't very good so when it rained the street would flood with water. Did we let that stop us? No! My brother and I would put on our rainboots and splash around in the knee deep water – simple pleasures.

Eventually, Mom and Dad bought us a basketball net for **our** driveway. Our direct neighbour, an older white man, didn't like that. He came out yelling at us, saying we were setting it up too close to his home, and that he didn't want kids like us playing by his house – long story short, he moved.

I knew right then and there how important image was. It wasn't some conceited notion or a way of showing off, but our safety. If we could project the "perfect" family with well-managed kids and a clean home, then we could change thoughts about Black people. My dad made sure we learned this lesson young for when the time comes to buy our own homes; he didn't want people doubting our homeownership or ability to maintain a good home. But sometimes it doesn't matter what we do, or how different we're not. That's their problem though, not ours, not yours.

I think my parents hoped I was too little to understand why he moved away. But when you're surrounded by people who don't look like you, you tend to become hyper aware – for protection. I knew though, I mean, he said it to us: he didn't want Black people as neighbours.

My Dear Black Girl,

We've had to grow up quickly. Those are only a couple of the early childhood lessons that made me grow quicker than my peers, that made me the "mature" kid – the "mom" of the friend group. We might not have the ability to play on our front lawns without worrying that our neighbours will stereotype us or that our actions will leave a bad impression on how they see future Black kids – and I hope this has changed in the 16 years since I was a kid – but know that these early childhood lessons are the reason you're formidable, compassionate, and you. From here, you can begin to gain the strength to claim your power.

Let It Go, Leave It Here

Have you ever had to code-switch? What did it feel like?

Let It Go, Leave It Here

Did you feel like you had to mature faster than others? How did that responsibility make you feel?

CHAPTER 2
HIDING MY ROOTS,
LOSING MY RHYTHM

"When we speak, we are afraid our words will not be heard
or welcomed. But when we are silent, we are still afraid.
So it is better to speak."
– Audre Lorde

I hope on the journal pages before this chapter you were
able to write down what you were feeling or that you
shared your story too. An important part of this journey
is that you take the time to reflect so that when you look
back on those pages, you can see how much you've grown
and see how strong you are. Thank you. I can feel how
much you've held onto – take a deep breath. Hold. One.
Two. Three. Exhale. Let it go, leave it here.

In the next few chapters, I'm going to bring you through
what it was like for me in elementary school. I'll start
by saying that I loved it. The school itself, the teachers,

my friends, and the memories I have. But as I've gotten older, I've realized there was a lot more on my mind then I realized at the time. And I'll tell you now – all the doubts I had, the loneliness I felt at times, or the questioning of myself that I did – didn't take away from all the fun and laughter there was too.

More Than Just Lunch

My favourite food as a kid was my mom's bully beef and rice. She cooked the bully beef in white rice with Lipton that added some noodles and chicken broth (sorry to give away your recipe, Mom). Other favourites: jerk chicken, pig tail soup, rice and peas (a.k.a. "red rice"), plantain, ackee and saltfish, fungi – maybe I should stop there before we both get too hungry.

None of my friends would have ever known those were my favourite foods. Those are foods that represent my heritage and the love my parents had for me that they poured into each ingredient and step of the cooking process. They'd never know because I never brought them to school or invited them over for dinner.

Partly because it was easier to make a sandwich that didn't need to be warmed up, and partly because it was easier to bring a thermos of Campbell's soup, but also because I didn't want any questions. It's cliché, I know, but t's a cliché for a reason. I didn't want to hear, "What's that smell?" or "Ew what did you bring for lunch?"

I remember when we had an international potluck. Each kid chose a country and then had to bring a food to represent that culture. I seized the opportunity to share a piece of my culture through food. My aunt from Antigua was visiting – how perfect! And, so, she made me some fungi.

Fungi - [foon-gee]

noun

National dish of Antigua and Barbuda. Made from cornmeal and Okra.

Other kids brought pasta, pizza, someone brought Jiaozi dumplings (which were so good by the way), and someone else made sushi rolls out of Fruit Roll Ups, Gushers, and Rice Krispies. **No one** ate the fungi. I was sad and hurt; it felt like rejection. It wouldn't be until I was 17 years old that I would build the courage to invite my best friend to a family dinner and feel proud to show her what I *actually* eat. Until then, any time someone came over, it was burgers, hot dogs, or pizza. I broke my own heart. I tucked away pieces of me, and as I said in the previous chapter – being Caribbean is the essence of who I am.

I wish I learned this sooner, but sharing more of my culture, not less, brought me and my true friend closer together. She tries everything – and without judgement, without pause. I don't think I've ever said how much that meant to me. Hiding who you are takes too much energy, too much time, time that is better spent hanging out with your friends, chasing your passions, and as a role model, I should probably say doing homework.

My Dear Black Girl,

It is not a small thing to share who you are through food. Food is a great connector for many people and many cultures, and sometimes is the best way to get to know someone. What does it matter that someone doesn't like your lunch? Who cares? You like it. Food does more than feed your body; it feeds your soul and is an expression of who you are.

Offbeat and Out of Place

Music is also a great unifier. Every culture has music that speaks to their spirit and expresses who they are. For me, that was the soca, reggae, calypso, and dancehall (in retrospect maybe I shouldn't have been listening to dancehall so young) that poured from my home and helped me learn about my heritage. I thank artists like Alison Hinds, Bob Marley, Machel Montano, Bunji Garlin, Elephant Man, and Patrice Roberts – I can go on, but I thank them for bringing me home to the islands and peeking into the childhoods of my parents.

When I felt lost, I spent hours on the family computer curating playlists and ripping them onto CDs, and, when it came out, the iPod was my best friend. I would sometimes sit in my room on the floor, eyes closed, and listen to my dad's music from his sound system in the living room below, feeling the vibrating floor and getting lost in the singers' stories. Here's a hack – your bathroom has the best acoustics; if you can, get a speaker in your bathroom, or put your phone in the sink and immerse yourself in the musical experience.

Music was and is my escape – my peace; but at a certain point in my life, I lost sight of that. Sometimes you feel torn between two cultures – that of your parents and that of your peers.

I listened to the radio every morning before school, a top 40 radio station that played the latest hits, but what I wasn't hearing was soca, reggae, calypso, or dancehall; I was hearing, pop, rap, country, and rock. I couldn't relate.

At sleepovers, sometimes my friends would play music for us to dance or sing to and I faked it. I mimicked their moves or mumbled the few words I knew. And maybe you're sensing a theme at this point in my story, but of course, I *never* played them my music – I definitely didn't think they'd understand patois, let alone like it; and let's be honest, I didn't want to spend my time translating.

So, here we are again, another time of my life where it might have seemed like something small or with little impact, but it's the small things that stand out most. I felt on the outside looking in. Quickly, Alison Hinds was replaced by Nicki Minaj, Bob Marley by Chris Brown, Machel Montano by Avril Lavigne, Bunji Garlin by Usher, Elephant Man by Eminem, and Patrice Roberts by P!nk. Don't get me wrong, I love those artists, and they make some bangers, but they served more for me to fit in than to express myself. Yeah, I could sing *Sk8ter Boy* like nobody's business but I felt like I was living as two people – the Lyrique who listened to top 40 with her friends and the Lyrique who listened to Soca Gold 2004 with her parents; and no, the two worlds wouldn't collide for a long time.

It's not *just* music or *just* clothes or *just* food or *just*... whatever – these are pieces of you, beautiful you. If your playlist is full of your cultural music, wonderful; if it's full of top 40, amazing; if it's a mix of both, great – you should feel proud to hit shuffle on your music library and not be embarrassed of what song might come on, no matter your audience.

My Dear Black Girl,

Few things I'm going to tell you are not possible, but here's something that is: You *can't* be authentically yourself if you're living two lives. Trying to live that way, you'll eventually deceive yourself and you won't recognize your own reflection. Who you are at home and with your friends should be the same, and I know it'll take a while to get there, that's ok. But people can't love you for who you are if you're not your whole self.

Let It Go, Leave It Here

Were there moments when you wished you could hide parts of your culture? What made you feel that way?

Let It Go, Leave It Here

Have you ever felt torn between your culture and your friends?

CHAPTER 3
CURLS IN CHAOS: BONNETS, BRAIDS, AND AWKWARD QUESTIONS

"I've come to realize that beauty is not a standard; it's an idea. We can make our own rules, we can define our beauty. And it starts with how we love ourselves."
– Lupita Nyong'o

I have to say, from my early life until now, there have been tremendous strides in the Black hair community. Black hair is being seen and taken care of in a powerful way. There are lots of Black-owned brands in big name stores that cater directly to us and are devoted to taking care of every kink and curl. Even so, have you ever noticed how they're usually on small little stand alone shelves – separated from the other hair care?

Something to think about.

When I was a kid there was very little representation in the beauty and hair care space. I remember the only Black girls I saw on beauty store packaging were on those *Just for Me* or *ORS Olive Oil* relaxer boxes. So, I assumed that Black girls with relaxed hair were more beautiful. My mom wouldn't let me relax my hair (she had very bad experiences with it when she was that age), but that didn't matter to me; I wanted to be like girls on the boxes.

Going to the hair care store was an overwhelming experience. Wigs, weaves, braiding hair, gels, creams, relaxers – and no idea where to start.

My earliest memory of my relationship to my hair is me sitting on the floor between my mom's legs as she put my hair in braids. My favourite style she did was small simple braids that made me feel like I had long flowing hair like I saw on TV. I never wanted anyone else but my mom to do my hair; I would kick and scream if anyone else even tried.

I didn't know why at the time but every night I would go to bed with a red cap on my head. The cap was too big so we'd tie an elastic on the front to tighten it and make sure it wouldn't slip off in my sleep. I wore bubble elastics – you know the ones that would click and clack as you move; I wore butterfly clips – of course always matching my outfit; and I wore headbands – in part to hide my big forehead (as a kid you would never catch me without a headband).

The headbands served another purpose though. All the cool girls in my school wore headbands, especially the elastic TNA ones. Headbands meant that even with my braids and bubbles I could rock their hairstyles. My friends and I, when we were old enough, would go to the mall, what seems like weekly, head to *Claire's*, and buy a surprise bag. There were always headbands in there. And so my collection only grew.

The headbands allowed me to fit in (or so I thought). I was so afraid that someone could tell me apart from my peers. I'll take this opportunity to remind you that I grew up in Orléans, and it wasn't hard for me to stand out. From a young age I did what I could to blend in.

Hair, Water, and the Fear of Being Different

As a kid, I took swimming lessons – and I'm talking young, maybe from age 5 to 7. It was really important, for my dad especially, that my brother and I learned to swim since he suffers from cramps and one of his worst fears is that my brother or I are swimming, get a cramp, and not know how to help ourselves.

Now, most people usually take swimming lessons for longer than I did, since it takes more than two years to master the art, but I couldn't take it anymore. Every time I had to get ready for swimming, out came the swim cap.

At my young age I was already comparing myself to others, feeling so insecure and embarrassed. The white kids didn't have to wear a swim cap – their hair floated in the water, flowing behind them like Ariel or Aquamarine. I mean, who ever heard of a mermaid wearing a swim cap?

Let's be real, swim caps are horrible to put on anyways, every strand getting caught, the tight squeeze on your head, and the clumps of hair that came out when you used all your strength to rip it off (again, not a master swimmer so maybe there were easier ways).

My worst nightmare was being invited to a pool party at a friend's house because then they'd see me in a swim cap – another reason I'd stand out, and back then I certainly didn't want to stand out anymore.

For the same reason, I dreaded sleepovers because that meant the red cap. I felt silly. My friends could just tie their hair up in a messy bun or sleep with their hair all loose, but there I was with my elastic-tied red cap, looking like a strange unicorn. So, I would risk it. The beautiful braids my mom took hours to do and the accessories she carefully placed like jewels on a crown were ruined in one night's sleep.

My Dear Black Girl,

Every part of you should be celebrated, and most importantly by you. Your hair holds history, stories, and power. We can do so much with our hair that you've yet to discover. From the bald and beautiful - like the Dora Milaje in *Black Panther*, a mighty group of all female warriors, to long flowing curls – because yes, Black women can have long hair. But remember, there's no such thing as "good hair." Don't worry; we're going to talk about that too.

Hiding My Crown

I remember once walking down the stairs in elementary school, I think we were heading outside for recess, and a kid behind me said, "Your hair..." (I thought I was about to get a compliment) "... looks like little snakes." The beautiful braids I loved so much, my favourite hairstyle, was tainted. Thinking back, from then on I did everything I could to hide my natural hair.

Remember how I said I wouldn't let anyone else but my mom touch my hair? Well, when I got older, I made a special exception: my cousin – a hairdresser. She specializes in Black hair: wigs, weaves, braiding, gels, creams, relaxers, so, what was once overwhelming soon became clear.

Enter braided extensions (a.k.a braids).

Braids would now become my new style; my hair wouldn't be seen for maybe another decade, and I made sure of that. I now know that braids are a **protective** style, but back then I used them to hide my hair. I didn't know how to take care of my hair. To me it was unruly and untameable, so I relied heavily on braids.

Braids allowed me to get away with sleeping without the dreaded red cap or a bonnet for a couple of nights; I could throw my hair into a messy bun or have it flowing behind me as I swam. I would also use the braids to showcase a little more of myself and my style. I had every colour of braids under the sun – yellow, white, blue, green, red, purple, silver, blue and green at the same time – anything that would express the inner me. I felt good.

Best believe I still rocked those headbands, even more now that I had the long hair like my friends. I would even ask my cousin to cornrow half my hair so that I could mimic the shaved-side look. I was finally starting to feel like I fit in. But even with the new found confidence braids gave me, I still would feel waves of shame and embarrassment – everyone knew it wasn't my *"real"* hair.

I can't tell you the number of times someone would grab my hair when I walked by, ask if it was my real hair or ask how long *my* hair was compared to the braids. I would get asked all the time why I wore braids or if it was because I actually didn't have any hair of my own – and not just by kids. So, eventually, I stopped wearing the braids down altogether; they were always up in a bun, ponytail, or half-up, half-down style as my attempt to avoid those questions. Did that work? Of course not.

If I was getting all these questions with braids, what kind of questions would I get with my hair? I didn't even want to dare find out. For the rest of elementary school and all through highschool – braids.

My Dear Black Girl,

We can do so much with our hair from braids to 'fros. It only matters that your style makes *you* feel good. That will be hard to remember sometimes, but, when you forget, just think about how nothing can possibly compare to the crown you carry.

Let It Go, Leave It Here

Have you ever compared yourself to someone else?
What did you tell yourself in those moments,
and how did it make you feel?

Let It Go, Leave It Here

Have you ever felt embarrassed or ashamed of your natural hair?

CHAPTER 4
LOVE, IDENTITY AND
UN-BELONGING

"I don't think you can truly love someone until you
learn to love yourself."
– Erykah Badu

For this next part of my story I'm going to talk about
something I've only said out loud a handful of times.

When you're in your pre-teens and teens, much of your
life is about love and dating – maybe more than you
realize. Yes, it's at a young age, but the reality is you're
thinking about it. The teens in your TV shows are going
through dating drama that gets you hooked; I mean for
me when Raven and Devon were getting ready to on their
date to the Blue Rain concert in *That's So Raven*, oh my
gosh, or when Logan and Quinn finally got together in
Zoey 101, oh and how can we forget when Teddy found
out that Spencer was cheating on her with Skylar on *Good*

Luck Charlie (honourable mention: Kim and Ron's friends to lovers storyline in *Kim Possible*, wow).

These are kids' shows!

We're exposed very young to some heavy dating drama and we get invested in these characters and their love stories. We believe we should be having the same experiences as the characters. And, so, we too are consumed by the idea of love.

Melanin Matching

It's common to hear things like "Kim and Ron, sitting in a tree, K-I-S-S-I-N-G" on the playground or kids talking about who's got a crush on who. Honestly, sometimes it felt like school was a long dating show. We all know that one kid on the playground playing matchmaker running around trying to set you up with someone else or trying to figure out who likes who.

Now, when you're one of only a few Black kids in your grade the same thing always happens. No matter how old you are, everyone thinks you and the other Black kid would make "such a *cute* couple, awwww!"

We're taught as kids to match like things. The square peg goes in the square hole and the yellow ball goes in the yellow bucket, but it doesn't stop there. We seek these patterns everywhere, even though we might not be aware. So, of course to the playground kids it makes sense that the Black kids should be together.

Here's how that made me feel: I could only be beautiful or desirable to a Black boy.

It affected me more than I thought at the time. At 12 years old, I was ok with being single and alone for the rest of my life. If the non-Black *and* Black boys didn't want me, what were my chances as I got older? Instead, I shifted my focus to being "the friend."

There were two times in elementary school when a boy let me know that they had a crush on me and neither of them were Black, but by that time I was already so pessimistic because of the melanin matching and being one of the only kids who hadn't dated anyone that I felt almost pitied or like a last resort. They didn't directly make me feel this way, especially one who I would eventually date, but I knew there was a huge part of me that would always second guess my beauty and desirability.

It was easier to be "the friend." I could give others advice or lend them an ear when they needed it. Honestly, it's probably why I'm such a good listener now, and in hindsight I would not have wanted their drama at that young age, but it took me a long time from there to see myself as any kind of cute, pretty, or beautiful. There were moments, but they were fleeting.

My Dear Black Girl,

I think I'm still affected by the feelings of un-belonging. I don't ever tell myself that I'm beautiful; it feels strange to talk about myself that way. But, here's what I offer to you: *You are BEAU-TIFUL*. You know what, let's do an exercise together right now. Say this out loud:

I am beautiful. I am beautiful in all that I am.
I am beautiful because of everything that makes me, me.

Watching from the Sidelines

I often felt like I was watching from the sidelines. My friends (reminder, we're in Orléans so mostly all white) were deep in the dating game. At sleepovers we would talk about crushes and send prank texts. We would talk about it on the playground, on MSN, and let's be honest, in class – we were consumed. My white friends would be in on again, off again relationships, and I can say now that yeah, I was jealous from time to time.

The only thing that I could tell was different about me, compared to my friends – I'm Black.

I convinced myself that the reason no one wanted to be

with me was because they found the white girls more attractive, or worse, that as a Black girl, I was ugly in comparison. This feeling was entirely internalized. Not once did someone call me ugly (at least that I know of) or tell me that I was less than someone else.

My brother dated in school though; he dated white girls. I know that his grade was even more white than mine, but seeing my Black brother be with white girls made me feel even more that people think white women are more beautiful than Black women.

So, what did I do? I changed my look, again. Not only did my braids imitate their hairstyles, but I went from my tomboyish street style to more Pinterest-girly. I'd like to say I did it for myself and I was experimenting with my look, but, no; I did it to make myself more white. I was slowly erasing my identity.

Ask my mom. I used to throw a tantrum whenever she tried to put me in a dress growing up – I only wanted to wear my brother's hand-me-downs, and my shorts were never higher than the top of my knee. But, now, I was wearing as much *La Senza Girl* as I could. Short plaid shorts in every colour, tighter fitting tops, and dresses made more appearances than before. I wasn't comfortable, and I hated the way I was so consumed with my appearance.

My Dear Black Girl,

The last thing I want for you is to worry about your outfit more than your heart. A lot of people will tell you that looks don't matter, but allow me to be a little controversial here: They do. I know your looks matter to you. We all go through it. Caring too much about how we look to others. Try thinking this way instead – it helps a little:

Do *you* like your shirt? Your pants? Dress? Do *you* like how that colour looks on you? Perfect. Then that's what matters.

Care about how you look to you. Let me be the cautionary tale. It took me a long time to find myself again. Trends come and go, and we all follow them, but do it your own way. There's only one you; don't fade away into the crowd.

Let It Go, Leave It Here

What messages have you received—directly or
indirectly—about your beauty and worth?
How have those messages shaped the
way you see yourself?

Let It Go, Leave It Here

Have you ever felt like you weren't beautiful?
How did that feeling affect the way you carried yourself or interacted with others?

CHAPTER 5
HEARING THE DRUMBEATS
OF UNITY

Ubuntu – "I am because we are."

Whew, that was a lot. You can feel how much *I've* held onto, so, let's do this again – take a deep breath. Hold. One. Two. Three. Exhale. Let it go, leave it here.

I promise from here the tides will turn. After all, this book *is* about claiming your power. I want you to know what's ahead for you when you step into your being and become authentically you.

In this second half of the book I'm going to offer you what helped me become as confident and sure of myself as I am today. It's an ongoing practice but a journey I look forward to being on nonetheless.

Let's take a moment to talk about what claiming your power means.

To me, it means no longer comparing myself to others, knowing and acknowledging my worth, not seeking validation from anyone else, respecting and honouring my beauty and presence, and above all else, stepping into being the strong Black woman I am. The strong Black woman you are destined to become.

Let's dive back in.

Confidence in Motion

When I was 8 years old my parents asked me if I wanted to go back to swimming lessons or try dance. Can you guess what I chose? Well, choosing dance set my life on a whole new path.

My parents signed me up for Afro-Caribbean dance.

I had no idea what was in store. "Afro-Caribbean dance" I knew what those words meant but I didn't know what it looked like or how it felt. When I got there, it was above a ballet studio, so immediately I was like: "Oh, so these are dancers who've been training for years. There's no way I can do this." But my mom and I walked up a couple of flights of stairs, bust open the doors Kuzco-style, and we were greeted by probably the highest number of Black women I had ever seen in one place. I instantly relaxed, turned off my white voice and walk, and became Lyrique.

Spoiler alert: Dance and my dance teacher played a huge role in claiming my power.

I wasn't a shy kid, by any means, but being surrounded by so many strong Black women and girls made me a little hesitant. I knew two of the other girls in my dance class were from Orléans but went to a different school, and through talking I found out that a couple of others were from Orléans as well, but the majority of the girls were from Ottawa South.

Those Ottawa South girls commanded the room; they took to the dances right away, even coming up with their own routines. Now, I know it's because they had been with the studio for years, but then, I questioned whether I was Black enough. For the first time I truly felt like an "Orléans girl."

Again, no one directly made me feel this way or said anything to me – in fact we were an instant community. But here I was comparing myself to girls I thought were prettier, funnier, bolder, and more connected to their Blackness than me. By this age my Blackness was connected only to the colour of my skin; I had lost so much of my culture trying to fit in, but I was seeing these girls connect their Blackness to art, food, music, clothes, and dance, like I once did, and desperately wanted to do again.

So, you know what I did? Gave my all to Afro-Caribbean dance. No longer was it three words put together but it was a call home, a call to family and to unity. For the first time I was hearing other people talk like me. Our teacher even made us pay a $2 fine if we came to class ashy! Sounds like a silly thing but she was teaching us to respect our beautiful Black skin.

She went the extra mile for us. When I was about 14, she organized the Afro-Caribbean Cotillion of which I am a proud Alumna. She wanted to give us Black kids of African and Caribbean descent an opportunity to enter high society, which was historically not afforded to us. We had mentors and role models from the Black community guiding us through the program; we took etiquette classes, had dressing for success talks, and participated in the much appreciated Ask a Brother, Ask a Sister session.

Ask a Brother, Ask a Sister was our chance to sit with kids our age of the opposite sex and have an honest conversation and ask what we wanted to know. The question that stood out to me most: Do Black boys prefer weaves, wigs, or natural hair?

Their response: We prefer whatever makes her most confident.

At the end of the Cotillion program there was a grand ball. No, we didn't waltz; we did a formal dance to reggae: *She's Royal* by Tarrus Riley.

"And when they ask what a good woman's made of. She's not afraid and ashamed of who she is. She's royal."
- Tarrus Riley

I knew this song before Cotillion but now it had a new meaning. I was afraid and ashamed of who I was – and I wasn't the woman I wanted to be. To become her, I could no longer feel the fear and shame I had about myself.

My Dear Black Girl,

I am a proud Afro-Caribbean dancer of ten years. It's important to find your community, people who understand what you're going through, and if you can't find it, build it. It can start with a book club, a bowling team, a music group, or, like me, with dance. I promise that when you can see pieces of yourself reflected in your community, you'll begin to see the best parts of you reflected back, and that's only the beginning.

Who's Got Aux?

Because of dance I was reintroduced to the music that once brought me peace and comfort. Weekly I was hearing soca, reggae, calypso, dancehall, and more – not just in my home or headphones, but out loud with kids my age. My love for music was back with a force. I couldn't keep it in anymore; it had to be shared.

So, for my elementary school talent show, I got three of my friends – white girls – to do a dance with me. I chose *Blazin* by Alison Hinds, the finale song we did every year at the dance recital, the song that reawakened my soul.

For the last few counts of our talent show performance we asked the whole school to get up and do the routine with us. We had everyone dancing – to soca!

That was the first time my friends heard music from my culture and heritage and I was hooked on that feeling. I was no longer weighed down by shame or embarrassment and was instead radiating pride. A piece of Lyrique shone through that day and was never dulled again.

Flash forward. To high school. When I could, I would plug my precious iPod into the cafeteria speaker system and play *my* music! Me and some other girls (Black girls!) would make a dance circle during lunch and create a vibe that was for everyone but connected *us* and allowed *us* to take a whole lunch period to honour our backgrounds.

And when I got my license and could drive to school, you best believe I was that kid with the windows down, trunk shaking, trying to make the whole city hear my music. After all, I am my father's daughter; I mean, the man had a subwoofer and tuned up speaker system in his car.

My Dear Black Girl,

If anything I share in this book sticks with you, I hope it's this:

When you are proud of who you are,
who you are becomes unstoppable.

Let It Go, Leave It Here

What is one belief about yourself that you are ready to let go of? What new truth do you want to embrace instead?

Let It Go, Leave It Here

When do you feel most like yourself? What environments, people, or activities help you feel free and authentic?

CHAPTER 6
QUARANTINE CROWN:
WASH DAY EPIPHANIES

"When I think of my hair, I think of strength and heritage.
It's part of my power as a Black woman."
– Danai Gurira

2020.

Quarantine.

Let's not take too much time talking about that – you've either lived through it or you're reading this years after and it's in your history books. I had just gotten my first sew-in wig. A cute little curly bob that had me feeling myself. But now, we were in lockdown, unable to socialize with anyone outside our households or even go to non-essential stores.

After a few days I was **READY** to get that wig off my head. I had never worn anything like it and it was feeling tight and itchy. I was too scared to take it off myself because that meant cutting through thin thread, the same colour as my hair, when I couldn't really see. I took the risk and got the wig off. But now it was my natural hair and me.

I didn't own many hair care products. I always went to my cousin for help. All I had was my shower, some combs, and *Mane n' Tail* shampoo and conditioner.

YouTube University

Luckily, I knew how to cornrow my own hair. I was pretty good at it too, so I had a hairstyle in mind for after my first solo shampoo and condition. This was the first time I handled my hair under running water, so I'd never felt what my hair was like in that state. I got lost in it. Running my hands through every knot and clump, carefully conditioning and pulling them apart until they became kinks and curls. I had a little Ariel moment in there – it was a whole new world, one that my thirsty hair was craving.

I *needed* to learn more. To learn how to keep my hair healthy and see what it can do. I put my hair in straight back cornrows and headed right to YouTube. I saw Black women talking about hair type, texture, and porosity, but I wasn't overwhelmed. I was fueled by curiosity.

Very quickly my YouTube subscriptions were all my new hair care coaches, there for me whenever I needed. And I had a lot of catching up to do. With nothing else to do but stay in my room, I absorbed all that I could. I learned that I have type 4B hair and low porosity, which equipped me with the knowledge of products that might work best for me. They taught me different hairstyles I could do: bantu knots, twist-outs, braid-outs, wash-and-gos, flat twists, and more! I experimented with all of them to find my signature: twist-outs.

I even gained the confidence to dye my hair! In retrospect, I should've waited until I could see a professional, but quarantine boredom was hitting hard.

I hard-launched my natural hair on Instagram – a huge step for me as pretty much everyone on there had never seen my hair before. I felt safer doing it this way. I could just not look at comments or not worry about the like count, so that even if someone said my hair looked like snakes, my new favourite hairstyle couldn't be tainted.

I found myself a part of another Black community who understood me and didn't make me feel guilty for not knowing how to do my hair. They openly shared their own struggles and the anxiety of deciding to wear your natural hair in a world that is yet to embrace it. I had always heard talk of Black hair being unacceptable in the workplace or inappropriate at formal events – inappropriate anywhere in public really – but the women I was now following on YouTube dashed all the negativity away and wore their crowns with honour.

My Dear Black Girl,

To this day I continue to wear my natural hair. Since my wash day epiphany I no longer see my hair as unruly or untameable; it's gorgeous. I encourage you to take the time to learn about Black hair. It's knowledge worth having. For me, it empowered me to take care of myself through self-love, self-care, and self-respect.

R.e.s.p.e.c.t.

"Good hair." Let's talk about it. So often we hear, "Oh, she's got good hair" or "I wish I had good hair like you," but what some don't see is how **demoralizing**, **painful**, and **downright ridiculous** the concept of "good hair" is.

When I first started wearing my natural hair out, it was chin-length, undefined, and voluminous. I had shedding and shrinkage – all the things that signified my hair was healthy and thriving – but I rarely got compliments. The longer I kept doing my natural hair, the longer it got, the more defined my zig-zag pattern became, and the more voluminous it appeared. As soon as my curl pattern started to pop, I started to hear, "Wow, you've got the good hair."

Let me give you another example from the TV show *Girlfriends*. *Girlfriends* did a lot for Black women; we were seeing the lives of 4 successful Black women and a cast of primarily Black actors. But when Toni Childs (one of the women) and her white husband got pregnant, talk of "good hair" came up frequently. Toni was excited that her baby would have "good hair" unlike her because the father is white, and Veretta (Toni's mother) claimed that she would be a Black child *with* good hair.

As hard, uncomfortable, and triggering it is to hear them talk like that in the show, it unfortunately reflects our real world.

So, why is "good hair" so hurtful? It's saying that kinky, coily, Black hair is undesirable, inferior, and bad. Anyone who doesn't have straight hair or loose curls or is mixed Black and white has "bad hair."

This is why so many Black women and girls feel like they can't take care of their hair or that it's not deserving of respect.

This is why it is so important that Black hair care brands are becoming more common and are getting into big name stores – accessible to all. Black women and girls have more options that cater to the needs of their hair than before, and it's just getting started. Creams, butters, gels; you name it.

My Dear Black Girl,

You are so much more than your hair, but hair *is* a big part of the Black community. Hair holds history and stories. It deserves to be taken care of and respected. Let's get rid of this concept of "good hair." We owe it to ourselves to stop comparing ourselves to other people. We are all unique, strong, powerful, and beautiful. Once I stopped comparing myself to others and convincing myself that I was less than, I began to see how truly special I am.

Let It Go, Leave It Here

What are some things you love about your hair's texture, versatility, or uniqueness? How can you celebrate those things more?

Let It Go, Leave It Here

Write 5 empowering words or affirmations you can speak over yourself daily, embracing your unique beauty and presence.

CHAPTER 7
REFLECTION TO RADIANCE

"All that you touch, you change.
All that you change changes you."
– Octavia Butler

Say it with me again:

I am beautiful. I am beautiful in all that I am. I am beautiful because of everything that makes me, me.

It may be difficult, but when you take the time to reflect on everything that got you to where you are today, you get to see all the things that made you radiant. When I reflect – all those moments of identity loss, feeling torn, self-doubt, shame, fear, embarrassment, dread – passion, community, and empowerment brought me to you and gave me the opportunity to create a safe space for us.

n these last chapters I'm going to share with you the things I tell myself every day, the things that keep me growing in beauty, strength, and power.

Rihanna Said it Best - Shine bright like a diamond

"Find light in the beautiful sea. I choose to be happy. You and I; we're like diamonds in the sky."
- Rihanna

've tried to describe to you how much music means to me, and I hope that message has come across. But I think t means more than *I* can even understand. But what Rihanna is saying in her song *Diamonds* has always stuck with me.

n all of the darkness that surrounds us, there's still beauty. We can choose light, choose to be happy, and when we do, we shine bright like a diamond. But, let's take that a step further. When you choose to be *you*, **YOU** shine bright like a diamond.

Think about it this way. You're the only one of you. Unique. Exceptional. So why would you want to be anyone else? There is strength in choosing to respect and honour your beauty every day and make it a habit.

Remember, it's ok to feel insecure or unsure sometimes – we all do. You're not alone, but you should know that *you* have the greatest power to uplift and embolden your being. The pain you feel is real. But it's only for a moment It'll pass.

My daily affirmation to remind me to shine bright (shoutout *Wreck-It-Ralph* for this one):

There's no one I'd rather be than me.

The Energy Budget

In your journey to claiming your power, it's equally important to protect your peace and your energy. I started by having "Selfish Saturdays," a day where, when possible, I wouldn't go anywhere or do anything for anyone else but me.

This allowed me to set boundaries with others and with myself. I learned what I can let go of to stop pushing myself too hard, especially when I didn't need to. But it taught me a secondary lesson: I have to treat myself with little luxuries. Luxury doesn't mean anything expensive or lavish; to me it was washing my hair and blasting a playlist on my bathroom speaker, doing my skin care routine, taking a nap to reset my brain, and catching up on TV.

Selfish Saturday was also a day to remember that I don't live for others; I live for me. It's important to give myself the time and attention that I give to everyone else.

There's another part to this energy budget.

We don't have enough time on this earth or energy in a lifetime to spend trying to hide who we are. When we live as our authentic selves, time seems to slow down. In my teens I came home too many times from school or work and dropped asleep in my bed exhausted, skipping dinner, sleeping until the next day because of code-switching or hiding away pieces of myself.

My daily affirmation to remind me not to waste my energy:

I don't have the time or energy to be anyone or anything else.

Let It Go, Leave It Here

What is one small thing you can do today to protect your peace?
How will you prioritize your well-being moving forward?

Let It Go, Leave It Here

Write down or draw 5 things you love about yourself.
How do each of these qualities make you feel when you think
about them?

CHAPTER 8
CLAIMING MY POWER

"If you want to fly, you have to give up the things
that weigh you down."
– Toni Morrison

How are you? Let me take this moment to check in with you. We've talked about a lot, so I want to make sure you've given yourself time to reflect and absorb. This book isn't just about me. It's about you, about how you're on your journey of becoming.

As Black girls we don't often have the luxury of just being a kid; we've got a lot on our minds from a world that is still learning to embrace and respect us. This book is about letting go –of the weight, the expectations, and the pain we carry. These pages allow me to hold some of that for you.

Last time. Take a deep breath. Hold. One. Two. Three. Exhale. Let it go, leave it here.

Wisdom in Embracing the Now

While it's tempting to look ahead and dream of the you you'll be in 20 years, it's necessary to live in the now. You don't want to miss the you you are. There's a point in your life when you'll look back and wish you had been more present, but then, you'd be missing the you you have become.

See the dangerous cycle?

You are your past, future, *and* present. So when your hands are busy grasping at what will be or what once was, you're neglecting what is, and you can't claim your power.

My daily affirmation to remind me to embrace the now:

I am who I am, when and where I am.

Power in Being Yourself

A lot of this book and much of my story is a journey of self-love. I lost my identity, was embarrassed by my culture, thought I was too Black and wasn't Black enough. I wanted to hide and fit in. I was sad and felt unwanted.

So, what did I do?

I **defined** my own identity.

I **embraced** my culture.

I **celebrated** my Blackness.

I **stood** out.

I **uplifted** my spirit.

I **chose** myself.

None of it happened overnight and I'm still working on it all, but letting go of those old thoughts and feelings freed up my being to step into my becoming.

My Dear Black Girl, let's do this together.

My daily affirmation to remind me to be myself:

I love you.

Let It Go, Leave It Here

How do you feel about yourself in this moment, without thinking about past mistakes or future expectations? What does your present self need from you today?

Let It Go, Leave It Here

What are some affirmations or positive thoughts you can remind yourself of when self-doubt creeps in? How can you make them part of your routine?

Be sure to check back on this page in times of self-doubt I'm here for you, I'm with you.

AUTHOR'S NOTE

"I am not afraid of being powerful and strong, and I think
that's the most beautiful thing I can do for myself."
– Beyoncé

Dear Black Girl,

Thank you for listening. These pages are always here for you
when you need – I'm always here for you. I know that this
was difficult, and I also know how freeing it is. Letting it go so
you're not weighed down by your thoughts. I hope you know
those doubts and questions are only for a moment.

Writing this book was my way of letting it all go. I already
believed I was a strong, powerful, inspirational, Black
woman, but I was carrying too much. Now that I've
shared, it's no longer holding me back, and I'm free to
flourish even more. As I'm writing this, I'm 26 years old. I've
always said 26 will be my golden year and it starts with
this book; it starts by chronicling my life in hopes that I
can help someone.

My dear, beautiful, strong, Black girl,

Let me hold your pain. You can't claim your power if your hands are full. The questions others ask you and the things they say may not be coming from a place of harm, but they still hurt – I know they make you question yourself; they made me. Letting go doesn't mean forgetting – all past things make you who you are today. Letting go means that you're not letting them define who you *can* be; that's still up to you to decide.

With love,

Lyrique Richards

ABOUT THE AUTHOR

Born and raised in Ottawa, Ontario, Canada, to immigrant parents from Jamaica and Antigua, Lyrique's Caribbean heritage is a cornerstone of her identity. From ten years as an Afro-Caribbean dancer to being an alumna of the Afro-Caribbean Cotillion program, she carries her culture proudly, using it to foster understanding and celebrate diversity.

A dog mom to her Yorki-Poo, Roscoe, and growing in life with her partner, Khaleel, Lyrique is passionate about uplifting her peers. She is dedicated to inspiring those around her to embrace their authenticity and potential. A natural storyteller, she uses her voice to encourage and empower others.

Guided by her mantra, "Just do you, and you'll leave your mark," Lyrique is determined to make an impact.

Instagram: @lyrique_richards
Website: https://www.lyriquerichards.ca
Email: hello@lyriquerichards.ca

thank you

Thank you for reading my book!

Dear Reader,

You made it! Thank you for giving me the space to share my story and for walking through my life. I hope this book gave you the space to share your story, the opportunity to reflect, and the confidence to claim your power. It means more than I can describe that we did this together.

Now, if I could ask a quick favour: if you enjoyed the book, would you mind leaving a positive review on Amazon or Goodreads? It would truly make my day, and it's one of the best ways to help others find this book and make my dream a reality. Your review might just be the encouragement someone else needs to empower them to step into their being.

With love,

Lyrique Richards

MY GIFT TO YOU

I am so glad you're here!

As my Gift to you, get FREE Access to the Audiobook of
Dear Black Girl, Let Me Hold Your Pain and other bonus content by
scanning the QR Code below or visiting
lyriquerichards.ca